This book belongs to

Brock

May God's Word bring you wisdom and strength in life. Always Chase Him!

—Spencer B

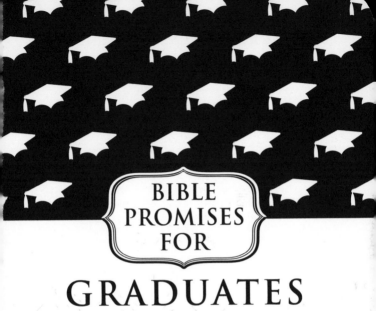

BIBLE PROMISES FOR

GRADUATES

BroadStreet
PUBLISHING

CONTENTS

DEVOTIONAL ENTRIES

INTRODUCTION

Congratulations! You've made it through a significant season of your life and many new adventures await you.

This Bible Promise book is designed to engage you in topics specific to what you face each day. As you embrace God's words of truth, be filled with joy, strength, wisdom, and renewed purpose for the day ahead. Gain confidence as you learn that the God who created you designed you for something special.

How can you be sure you are making the right choices? By placing your confidence and hope in the incredible goodness of God. He loves you just because you are his, and he is excited to show you his plan!

ABILITY

We are not saying that we can do this work ourselves. It is God who makes us able to do all that we do.

2 CORINTHIANS 3:5 NCV

Take a new grip with your tired hands and strengthen your weak knees. Mark out a straight path for your feet so that those who are weak and lame will not fall but become strong.

HEBREWS 12:12-13 NLT

"My grace is sufficient for you, for my power is made perfect in weakness." Therefore I will boast all the more gladly of my weaknesses, so that the power of Christ may rest upon me.

2 CORINTHIANS 12:9 ESV

We can rejoice, too, when we run into problems and trials, for we know that they help us develop endurance. And endurance develops strength of character, and character strengthens our confident hope of salvation. And this hope will not lead to disappointment. For we know how dearly God loves us, because he has given us the Holy Spirit to fill our hearts with his love.

ROMANS 5:3–5 NLT

After you have suffered for a little while, the God of all grace, who called you to His eternal glory in Christ, will Himself perfect, confirm, strengthen and establish you.

1 PETER 5:10 NASB

ACCEPTANCE

"The Father gives me the people who are mine. Every one of them will come to me, and I will always accept them."

JOHN 6:37 NCV

Before he made the world, God chose us to be his very own through what Christ would do for us; he decided then to make us holy in his eyes, without a single fault—we who stand before him covered with his love.

EPHESIANS 1:4 TLB

If God is for us, who can be against us?

ROMANS 8:31 ESV

"Here I am! I stand at the door and knock. If anyone hears my voice and opens the door, I will come in and eat with that person, and they with me."

REVELATION 3:20 NIV

"Do not be afraid, for I have ransomed you.
I have called you by name; you are mine.
When you go through deep waters,
I will be with you.
When you go through rivers of difficulty,
you will not drown.
When you walk through the fire of oppression,
you will not be burned up;
the flames will not consume you.
For I am the LORD, your God,
the Holy One of Israel, your Savior.
I gave Egypt as a ransom for your freedom;
I gave Ethiopia and Seba in your place.
Others were given in exchange for you.
I traded their lives for yours
because you are precious to me.
You are honored, and I love you."

ISAIAH 43:1–4 NLT

ADOPTION

You did not receive a spirit of slavery to fall back into fear, but you have received a spirit of adoption. When we cry, "Abba! Father!" it is that very Spirit bearing witness with our spirit that we are children of God.

ROMANS 8:15–16 NRSV

The LORD will not abandon His people on account of His great name, because the LORD has been pleased to make you a people for Himself.

1 SAMUEL 12:22 NASB

A father of the fatherless and a judge for
the widows, is God in His holy habitation.
God makes a home for the lonely;
He leads out the prisoners into prosperity.

PSALM 68:5-6 NASB

"I will not abandon you as orphans—
I will come to you."

JOHN 14:18 NLT

But when the right time came, God sent his Son,
born of a woman, subject to the law. God sent him
to buy freedom for us who were slaves to the law,
so that he could adopt us as his very own children.

GALATIANS 4:4-5 NLT

"I will bring the blind by a way they did not know;
I will lead them in paths they have not known.
I will make darkness light before them,
And crooked places straight.
These things will I do for them,
And not forsake them."

ISAIAH 42:16 NKJV

MADE ON PURPOSE

It was you who formed my inward parts;
you knit me together in my mother's womb.
I praise you, for I am fearfully
and wonderfully made.
Wonderful are your works;
that I know very well.

PSALM 139:13-14 NRSV

Even before you were born, the Lord was busy
working on you. God knew what color your eyes
were going to be, and how thick or thin or curly or
straight your hair would turn out. And even better,
he knew all the character traits that add up to
exactly what makes you, you!

Here's the best thing: God doesn't make mistakes.
What does that mean for you? It means that he

knew what he was doing with every trait he gave you. He thinks you are wonderful!

You may be questioning why you were born with such and such, or why you have this or that personality trait. But he made you that way on purpose, to use it for his glory, because he saw the beauty in you!

PRAYER:

Lord, help me to see how wonderfully you've made me, every day. You don't make mistakes. I want to believe that. You formed each part of me with your perfect design. I want to embrace my unique purpose and walk in all you have called me to.

ANXIETY

Be still in the presence of the LORD
and wait patiently for him to act.
Don't worry about evil people who prosper
or fret about their wicked schemes.
Stop being angry!
Turn from your rage!
Do not lose your temper—
it only leads to harm.

PSALM 37:7-8 NLT

Be still, and know that I am God.
I will be exalted among the nations,
I will be exalted in the earth!

PSALM 46:10 ESV

Do not be anxious about anything, but in every
situation, by prayer and petition, with thanksgiving,
present your requests to God.

PHILIPPIANS 4:6 NIV

In my trouble I cried to the L<small>ORD</small>,
And He answered me.

PSALM 120:1 NASB

I want them to be encouraged and knit together
by strong ties of love. I want them to have
complete confidence that they understand God's
mysterious plan, which is Christ himself.

COLOSSIANS 2:2 NLT

"I have told you all this so that you may have
peace in me. Here on earth you will have many
trials and sorrows. But take heart, because I have
overcome the world."

JOHN 16:33 NLT

13

ASSURANCE

Your promises have been thoroughly tested,
and your servant loves them.
My eyes stay open through the
watches of the night,
that I may meditate on your promises.

PSALM 119:140, 148 NIV

He has granted to us his precious and very great
promises, so that through them you may become
partakers of the divine nature, having escaped from
the corruption that is in the world.

2 PETER 1:3-4 ESV

To him who is able to do immeasurably more than
all we ask or imagine, according to his power that
is at work within us, to him be glory...for ever and
ever! Amen.

EPHESIANS 3:20-21 NIV

All of God's promises have been fulfilled in Christ with a resounding "Yes!"

2 CORINTHIANS 1:20 NLT

These things I have written to you who believe in the name of the Son of God, that you may know that you have eternal life, and that you may continue to believe in the name of the Son of God.

1 JOHN 5:13 NKJV

Jesus Christ is the same
yesterday and today and forever.

HEBREWS 13:8 NASB

The LORD always keeps his promises;
he is gracious in all he does.

PSALM 145:13 NLT

BEAUTY

I will praise You,
for I am fearfully and wonderfully made;
Marvelous are Your works,
And that my soul knows very well.

PSALM 139:14 NKJV

Don't be concerned about the outward beauty of
fancy hairstyles, expensive jewelry, or beautiful
clothes. You should clothe yourselves instead with
the beauty that comes from within, the unfading
beauty of a gentle and quiet spirit, which is so
precious to God.

1 PETER 3:3–4 NLT

The LORD doesn't see things the way you see them.
People judge by outward appearance,
but the LORD looks at the heart.

1 SAMUEL 16:7 NLT

"And why do you worry about clothes? See how the wild flowers grow. They don't work or make clothing. But here is what I tell you. Not even Solomon in all his royal robes was dressed like one of these flowers. If that is how God dresses the wild grass, won't he dress you even better? Your faith is so small! After all, the grass is here only today. Tomorrow it is thrown into the fire. So don't worry. Don't say, 'What will we eat?' Or, 'What will we drink?' Or, 'What will we wear?' People who are ungodly run after all those things. Your Father who is in heaven knows that you need them."

MATTHEW 6:27–29 NIRV

He has made everything beautiful in its time.

ECCLESIASTES 3:11 NIV

BELONGING

God chose us to belong to Christ before the world
was created. He chose us to be holy and without
blame in his eyes. He loved us.

EPHESIANS 1:4 NIRV

We know that all things work together for good to
those who love God, to those who are the called
according to His purpose.

ROMANS 8:28 NKJV

No eye has seen, no ear has heard,
and no mind has imagined
what God has prepared
for those who love him.

1 CORINTHIANS 2:9 NLT

You are a chosen people, a royal priesthood, a holy nation, God's special possession, that you may declare the praises of him who called you out of darkness into his wonderful light.

1 PETER 2:9 NIV

There is a time for everything,
and everything on earth has its special season.

ECCLESIASTES 3:1 NCV

If you are wise and understand God's ways, prove it by living an honorable life, doing good works with the humility that comes from wisdom.

JAMES 3:13 NLT

When you think of a wise person, is there anyone specific who comes to mind? What is it about that person that makes you think they are so wise? Certain qualities define a wise person. How they live their lives and *show* wisdom is the most important quality of all.

It's more than talk; it's their walk. Boasting about their greatness or knowledge doesn't do it. Twisting situations to put themselves in a better light certainly doesn't either.

Living a life that follows the example Christ
set is a great way to become wise. When we
are humble, ask for others' opinions, seek
knowledge, and live to serve, we find wisdom for
ourselves. Be wise and follow the Lord!

PRAYER:

Father, thank you for being the ultimate
giver of wisdom. I want to seek your
wisdom at every turn. I pray that I'd
resist the temptation to tell people how
knowledgeable I am. I pray I'd remain your
humble servant.

BLESSING

You prepare a feast for me
in the presence of my enemies.
You honor me by anointing my head with oil.
My cup overflows with blessings.

PSALM 23:5 NLT

Blessed be the God and Father of our Lord Jesus
Christ, who has blessed us in Christ with every
spiritual blessing in the heavenly places, even as he
chose us in him before the foundation of the world,
that we should be holy and blameless before him.

EPHESIANS 1:3–4 ESV

From his abundance we have all received one
gracious blessing after another.

JOHN 1:16 NLT

For the Lord God is our sun and our shield.
He gives us grace and glory.
The Lord will withhold no good thing
from those who do what is right.

PSALM 84:11 NLT

The Lord bless you, and keep you;
The Lord make His face shine on you,
And be gracious to you;
The Lord lift up His countenance on you,
And give you peace.

NUMBERS 6:24–26 NASB

BRAVERY

Blessed is the one who trusts in the Lord,
whose confidence is in him.
They will be like a tree planted by the water
that sends out its roots by the stream.
It does not fear when heat comes;
its leaves are always green.
It has no worries in a year of drought
and never fails to bear fruit.

JEREMIAH 17:7–8 NIV

"Let not your heart be troubled; you believe in God,
believe also in Me. In My Father's house are many
mansions.... I go to prepare a place for you. And if
I go and prepare a place for you, I will come again
and receive you to Myself; that where I am, there
you may be also."

JOHN 14:1-3 NKJV

"Don't worry about tomorrow. Tomorrow will worry about itself. Each day has enough trouble of its own."

MATTHEW 6:34 NIRV

Those who love me, I will deliver;
I will protect those who know my name.
When they call to me, I will answer them;
I will be with them in trouble,
I will rescue them and honor them.

PSALM 91:14-15 NRSV

CARE

The LORD directs the steps of the godly.
He delights in every detail of their lives.
Though they stumble, they will never fall,
for the LORD holds them by the hand.

PSALM 37:23–24 NLT

I am sure that neither death nor life, nor angels nor
rulers, nor things present nor things to come, nor
powers, nor height nor depth, nor anything else in
all creation, will be able to separate us from the
love of God in Christ Jesus our Lord.

ROMANS 8:38–39 ESV

He tends his flock like a shepherd:
He gathers the lambs in his arms
and carries them close to his heart;
he gently leads those that have young.

ISAIAH 40:11 NIV

Blessed be the Lord

Because He has heard the voice

of my supplication.

The Lord is my strength and my shield;

My heart trusts in Him, and I am helped;

Therefore my heart exults,

And with my song I shall thank Him.

PSALM 28:6-7 NASB

Show me the right path, O Lord;
Point out the road for me to follow.
Lead me by your truth and teach me,
for you are the God who saves me.
All day long I put my hope in you.
My eyes are always on the Lord,
For he rescues me from the traps of my enemies.

PSALM 25:4-5, 15 NLT

We rely pretty heavily on our GPS devices to show us where to go. If we don't pay close attention to what it's saying, it's easy to end up off track.

It's common sense to watch where you're going or you'll get tripped up. When it comes to walking with God, though, it's a different story. Instead of looking ahead and watching your every move, the Bible says to look directly at the Lord, every moment of your life. He'll keep you from whatever traps you may fall into.

Spend less time looking at the details of your life and more time with your eyes fixed on God. He is the ultimate GPS, and he will lead you exactly where you need to go. It's only when you take your eyes off him, that you'll fall right smack into the trap the enemy sets for you. Stay close to God for the best directions.

PRAYER:

Lord, thank you for directing me where to go and showing me what steps to take. Help me to keep my eyes fixed on you, so I don't miss a turn or end up in the wrong place. Lead me by your truth. I want to walk on the right path.

COMFORT

To all who mourn he will give:
beauty for ashes;
joy instead of mourning;
praise instead of heaviness.
For God has planted them like strong and
graceful oaks for his own glory.

ISAIAH 61:3 TLB

May your unfailing love be my comfort,
according to your promise to your servant.

PSALM 119:76 NIV

May our Lord Jesus Christ himself and God our
Father, who loved us and by his grace gave us
eternal comfort and a wonderful hope, comfort you
and strengthen you.

2 THESSALONIANS 2:16–17 NLT

Unless the LORD had helped me, I would soon have settled in the silence of the grave. I cried out, "I am slipping!" but your unfailing love, O LORD supported me. When doubts filled my mind, your comfort gave me renewed hope and cheer.

PSALM 94:17–19 NLT

Praise be to the God and Father of our Lord Jesus Christ, the Father of compassion and the God of all comfort.

2 CORINTHIANS 1:3 NIV

God's dwelling place is now among the people, and he will dwell with them. "He will wipe every tear from their eyes. There will be no more death" or mourning or crying or pain, for the old order of things has passed away.

REVELATION 21:3–4 NIV

COMMITMENT

Commit everything you do to the LORD.
Trust him, and he will help you.

PSALM 37:5 NLT

I have fought the good fight, I have finished the
course, I have kept the faith; in the future there is
laid up for me the crown of righteousness, which
the Lord, the righteous Judge, will award to me on
that day; and not only to me, but also to all who
have loved His appearing.

2 TIMOTHY 4:7 NASB

Therefore, my dear brothers and sisters, stand firm.
Let nothing move you. Always give yourselves fully
to the work of the Lord, because you know that
your labor in the Lord is not in vain.

1 CORINTHIANS 15:58 NIV

Commit your work to the LORD,
and your plans will be established.

PROVERBS 16:3 ESV

"Seek first the kingdom of God and His
righteousness, and all these things
shall be added to you."

MATTHEW 6:33 NKJV

"If any of you wants to be my follower, you must
turn from your selfish ways, take up your cross
daily, and follow me."

LUKE 9:23 NLT

CONFIDENCE

Be my rock of refuge,

to which I can always go;

give the command to save me,

for you are my rock and my fortress.

You have been my hope, Sovereign Lord,

my confidence since my youth.

PSALM 71:3, 5 NIV

This is the confidence that we have toward him,

that if we ask anything according to his will

he hears us. And if we know that he hears us

in whatever we ask, we know that we have the

requests that we have asked of him.

1 JOHN 5:14–15 ESV

I can do everything through Christ,

who gives me strength.

PHILIPPIANS 4:13 NLT

Let us then approach God's throne of grace with confidence, so that we may receive mercy and find grace to help us in our time of need.

HEBREWS 4:16 NIV

We can confidently say, "The Lord is my helper; I will not fear; what can man do to me?"

HEBREWS 13:6 ESV

I am confident of this very thing, that He who began a good work in you will perfect it until the day of Christ Jesus.

PHILIPPIANS 1:6 NASB

But if you remain in me and my words remain in you, you may ask for anything you want, and it will be granted!

JOHN 15:7 NLT

CONTENTMENT

Light is sweet.
People enjoy being out in the sun.
No matter how many years anyone might live,
let them enjoy all of them.

ECCLESIASTES 11:7–8 NIRV

"If God cares so wonderfully for wildflowers that
are here today and thrown into the fire tomorrow,
he will certainly care for you. Why do you have
so little faith? So don't worry about these things,
saying, 'What will we eat? What will we drink?
What will we wear?' These things dominate the
thoughts of unbelievers, but your heavenly Father
already knows all your needs. Seek the Kingdom of
God above all else, and live righteously, and he will
give you everything you need."

MATTHEW 6:30-33 NLT

I know what it is to be in need, and I know what it is to have plenty. I have learned the secret of being content in any and every situation, whether well fed or hungry, whether living in plenty or in want. I can do all this through him who gives me strength.

PHILIPPIANS 4:12-13 NIV

"Blessed are those who are humble.
They will be given the earth."

MATTHEW 5:5 NIRV

WISDOM IN WAITING

Everything is appropriate in its own time. But
though God has planted eternity in the hearts of
men, even so, many cannot see the whole scope
of God's work from beginning to end.

ECCLESIASTES 3:11 TLB

The Lord loves us like crazy. He guides us, provides
for us, and takes care of us. God has changed our
lives for the better. He takes away the ugliness of
our sin and makes us beautiful inside. He is open
to us in every way, attentively listening to all our
prayers. It's hard to imagine all that he has done
or is going to do.

Sometimes, it seems like we have to wait forever
for his answers. We want to know everything he
has planned right at this moment, but it's just not

meant to be. Through waiting, we can learn
patience, humility, and so much more.

Being made to wait doesn't reflect a lack of
interest or love on God's part. Rather, it's his
infinite wisdom that keeps us close to him, learning
to trust him even when everything is not clear.

PRAYER:

*Father, thank you that there's wisdom to
be found in waiting. You know why some
things are not right for me to have or do
right now. I want to trust your timing. Help
me to be patient while I am waiting for you
to show me the way.*

COOPERATION

Make me truly happy by agreeing wholeheartedly
with each other, loving one another, and working
together with one mind and purpose.

PHILIPPIANS 2:2 NLT

Be of the same mind toward one another. Do not
set your mind on high things, but associate with the
humble. Do not be wise in your own opinion.

ROMANS 12:16 NKJV

May the God of endurance and encouragement
grant you to live in such harmony with one another,
in accord with Christ Jesus, that together you may
with one voice glorify the God and Father of our
Lord Jesus Christ. Therefore welcome one another as
Christ has welcomed you, for the glory of God

ROMANS 15:5-7 ESV

I appeal to you, brothers and sisters, in the name of our Lord Jesus Christ, that all of you agree with one another in what you say and that there be no divisions among you, but that you be perfectly united in mind and thought.

1 CORINTHIANS 1:10 NIV

All of you be harmonious, sympathetic, brotherly, kindhearted, and humble in spirit; not returning evil for evil or insult for insult, but giving a blessing instead; for you were called for the very purpose that you might inherit a blessing.

1 PETER 3:8-9 NASB

COURAGE

Love the Lord, all you godly ones!
For the Lord protects those who are loyal to him,
but he harshly punishes the arrogant.
So be strong and courageous,
all you who put your hope in the Lord!

PSALM 31:23–24 NLT

"Be strong and courageous. Do not be frightened,
and do not be dismayed, for the Lord your God is
with you wherever you go."

JOSHUA 1:9 ESV

Even though I walk through the valley of the
shadow of death,
I fear no evil, for You are with me;
Your rod and Your staff, they comfort me.

PSALM 23:4 NASB

I eagerly expect and hope that I will in no way be ashamed, but will have sufficient courage so that now as always Christ will be exalted in my body, whether by life or by death.

PHILIPPIANS 1:20 NIV

May he give you the power to accomplish all the good things your faith prompts you to do.

2 THESSALONIANS 1:11 NLT

When I am afraid, I put my trust in you.
In God, whose word I praise—
in God I trust and am not afraid.

PSALM 56:3-4 NIV

CREATIVITY

Having then gifts differing according to the grace
that is given to us, let us use them.

ROMANS 12:6 NKJV

The heavens are telling of the glory of God; And
their expanse is declaring the work of His hands.

PSALM 19:1 NASB

O LORD, what a variety of things you have made!
In wisdom you have made them all.
The earth is full of your creatures.

PSALM 104:24 NLT

He has filled him with divine spirit, with skill,
intelligence, and knowledge in every kind of craft.

EXODUS 35:31 NRSV

Let the beauty of the LORD our God be upon us,
And establish the work of our hands for us.

PSALM 90:17 NKJV

A man's gift makes room for him
And brings him before great men.

PROVERBS 18:16 NASB

Do you see people skilled in their work?
They will work for kings, not for ordinary people.

PROVERBS 22:29 NCV

Be sure to use the abilities God has given you.

1 TIMOTHY 4:14 TLB

BETTER WAYS

"My thoughts are nothing like your thoughts,"
says the LORD.
"And my ways are far beyond anything
you could imagine."

ISAIAH 55:8 NLT

How many times has your life taken a turn in a
direction you just didn't like?

"God, what are you thinking?" you might say.

"How can this be your plan?"

Sometimes we try to work out things logically,
based on what we know. Yet the Lord tells us
that he doesn't think like we do. He's got a bigger
picture in mind. God knows what's best, even when
his best isn't at all obvious.

It's hard to trust his will when the end of the path isn't clear. It can be incredibly difficult to be patient and push through tough times. But God is wise, and he knows everything. His thoughts are not like ours, and that's a good thing! We can trust in his plan, his timing, and his goodness.

PRAYER:

Lord, I know your ways are better than mine. You have great things planned for me and I believe that you will show them to me. I love that you have something in store for me that is more than I could have ever imagined! I trust in your goodness today.

DELIGHT

Oh, the depth of the riches both of the wisdom
and knowledge of God! How unsearchable are His
judgments and unfathomable His ways!

ROMANS 11:33 NASB

Blessed are those who find wisdom,
those who gain understanding,
for she is more profitable than silver
and yields better returns than gold.
She is more precious than rubies;
nothing you desire can compare with her.
Long life is in her right hand;
in her left hand are riches and honor.
Her ways are pleasant ways,
and all her paths are peace.

PROVERBS 3:13–17 NIV

Every good gift and every perfect gift is from above,
coming down from the Father of lights with whom
there is no variation or shadow due to change.

JAMES 1:17 ESV

I will tell of the kindnesses of the LORD,
the deeds for which he is to be praised,
according to all the LORD has done for us...
according to his compassion and many kindnesses.

ISAIAH 63:7 NIV

"A good man's speech reveals the rich treasures
within him."

MATTHEW 12:35 TLB

DELIVERANCE

I waited patiently for the LORD;
he turned to me and heard my cry.
He lifted me out of the slimy pit,
out of the mud and mire;
he set my feet on a rock
and gave me a firm place to stand.
He put a new song in my mouth,
a hymn of praise to our God.
Many will see and fear the LORD;
and put their trust in him.

PSALM 40:1–3 NIV

The LORD hears his people
when they call to him for help.
He rescues them from all their troubles.

PSALM 34:17 NLT

The righteous person faces many troubles,
but the LORD comes to the rescue each time.

PSALM 34:19 NLT

My prayer is to you, O LORD.
At an acceptable time, O God,
in the abundance of your steadfast love answer
me in your saving faithfulness.
Deliver me from sinking in the mire;
let me be delivered from my enemies
and from the deep waters.
Answer me, O LORD,
for your steadfast love is good;
according to your abundant mercy, turn to me.

PSALM 69:13-14, 16 ESV

DEPRESSION

Finally, brothers and sisters, whatever is true, whatever is noble, whatever is right, whatever is pure, whatever is lovely, whatever is admirable—if anything is excellent or praiseworthy—think about such things.

PHILIPPIANS 4:8 NIV

Why am I so sad?
Why am I so upset?
I should put my hope in God
and keep praising him.

PSALM 42:11 NCV

You, O LORD, are a shield about me,
my glory, and the lifter of my head.

PSALM 3:3 ESV

God... comforts the depressed.

2 CORINTHIANS 7:6 NASB

He has delivered us from the power of darkness and conveyed us into the kingdom of the Son of His love.

COLOSSIANS 1:13 NKJV

You, LORD, are my lamp;
the LORD turns my darkness into light.

2 SAMUEL 22:29 NIV

You are a chosen people, a royal priesthood, a holy nation, God's special possession, that you may declare the praises of him who called you out of darkness into his wonderful light.

1 PETER 2:9 NIV

DETERMINATION

Be attentive to my words;

incline your ear to my sayings.

Let them not escape from your sight;

keep them within your heart.

Let your eyes look directly forward,

and your gaze be straight before you.

PROVERBS 4:20–21, 25 ESV

Let us draw near to God with a sincere heart and with the full assurance that faith brings. Let us hold unswervingly to the hope we profess, for he who promised is faithful.

HEBREWS 10:22–23 NIV

Your lovingkindness, O LORD, extends to the heavens,

Your faithfulness reaches to the skies.

PSALM 36:5 NASB

God is faithful. He will not allow the temptation to be more than you can stand. When you are tempted, he will show you a way out so that you can endure.

1 CORINTHIANS 10:13 NLT

I keep my eyes always on the LORD.
With him at my right hand, I will not be shaken.

PSALM 16:8 NIV

LORD, you are my God;
I will exalt you and praise your name,
for in perfect faithfulness
you have done wonderful things,
things planned long ago.

ISAIAH 25:1 NIV

LORD, you are my God;
I will exalt you and praise your name,
for in perfect faithfulness
you have done wonderful things.
You are a tower of refuge to the poor, O LORD,
a tower of refuge to the needy in distress.
You are a refuge from the storm
and a shelter from the heat.

ISAIAH 25:1, 4 NIV

If you tried to fill a book with all the good things
about God, the pages would never end. He is good,
kind, loving, generous, just, and fair. While it might
not like seem like that sometimes (after all, the
world is full of bad things), God is faithful and walks
alongside us in tough times as well as good times.

God is perfectly faithful. That means he never
forgets about you or leaves you behind. He sticks

with you and provides a place of safety and refuge whenever you need it.

God has a beautiful plan for your life. But he won't force that plan on you. Instead he loves you by giving you a choice—to follow his plan or leave it. He knows his plan is best. It bubbles up from a heart that loves you deeply and knows you intimately. Will you trust him?

PRAYER:

Lord, thank you for knowing every detail of my life and caring enough about me to plan each step. I declare that you are perfectly faithful and you will continue to do wonderful things in and around me. Thank you for being my tower of refuge.

DEVOTION

With all my heart I have sought You;

Do not let me wander from Your commandments.

Your word I have treasured in my heart,

That I may not sin against You.

Teach me, O LORD, the way of Your statutes,

And I shall observe it to the end.

PSALM 119:10–11, 33 NASB

"Seek first the kingdom of God and His righteousness, and all these things shall be added to you."

MATTHEW 6:33 NKJV

Stand firm. Let nothing move you. Always give yourselves fully to the work of the Lord, because you know that your labor in the Lord is not in vain.

1 CORINTHIANS 15:58 NIV

Commit your work to the LORD,
and your plans will be established.

PROVERBS 16:3 ESV

May God himself, the God of peace, sanctify you
through and through. May your whole spirit, soul
and body be kept blameless at the coming of
our Lord Jesus Christ. The one who calls you is
faithful, and he will do it.

1 THESSALONIANS 5:23–24 NIV

"If any of you wants to be my follower, you must
turn from your selfish ways, take up your cross
daily, and follow me."

LUKE 9:23 NLT

DILIGENCE

The plans of the diligent lead to profit
as surely as haste leads to poverty.

PROVERBS 21:5 NIV

To enjoy your work and to accept your lot in life—
that is indeed a gift from God. The person who does
that will not need to look back with sorrow on his
past, for God gives him joy.

ECCLESIASTES 5:20 TLB

In all the work you are doing, work the best you
can. Work as if you were doing it for the Lord, not
for people.

COLOSSIANS 3:23 NCV

Be diligent in these matters; give yourself wholly to
them, so that everyone may see your progress.

1 TIMOTHY 4:15 NIV

Wise words bring many benefits,
and hard work brings rewards.

PROVERBS 12:14 NLT

Finish the work, so that your eager willingness to
do it may be matched by your completion of it,
according to your means.

2 CORINTHIANS 8:11 NIV

Pay careful attention to your own work, for then
you will get the satisfaction of a job well done,
and you won't need to compare yourself to
anyone else. For we are each responsible for our
own conduct.

GALATIANS 6:4–5 NLT

ENCOURAGEMENT

Though an army besiege me,
my heart will not fear;
though war break out against me,
even then I will be confident.
One thing I ask from the LORD,
this only do I seek:
that I may dwell in the house of the LORD
all the days of my life,
to gaze on the beauty of the LORD
and to seek him in his temple.
For in the day of trouble
he will keep me safe in his dwelling.

PSALM 27:3-5 NIV

The humble will see their God at work and be glad.
Let all who seek God's help be encouraged.

PSALM 69:32 NLT

May the God who gives endurance and encouragement give you the same attitude of mind toward each other that Christ Jesus had.

ROMANS 15:5 NIV

We do not lose heart, but though our outer man is decaying, yet our inner man is being renewed day by day. For momentary, light affliction is producing for us an eternal weight of glory far beyond all comparison.

2 CORINTHIANS 4:16–17 NASB

Let us consider how to stir up one another to love and good works, not neglecting to meet together, as is the habit of some, but encouraging one another.

HEBREWS 10:24–25 ESV

INFLUENCING VOICES

Brothers and sisters, think about the things that are good and worthy of praise. Think about the things that are true and honorable and right and pure and beautiful and respected. Do what you learned and received from me, what I told you, and what you saw me do. And the God who gives peace will be with you.

PHILIPPIANS 4:8-9 NCV

There are many influences in this world, each one speaking to us in different ways. Sorting out which voices are good and bad can be confusing.

From time to time, it's helpful to pause and take a minute to ask, "What voice am I allowing to influence my life, my heart, and my mind?" Words are powerful. They can breathe life. Or they can cause death.

The verse above is the perfect guide for deciding what helpful and what's not. If something is true and noble and right, that voice will point us to Jesus and encourage us to live a life for him. If it's something lovely or excellent or praiseworthy, that influence will draw us close to God. Anything that doesn't fit in this category will pull us away from what he wants for us.

PRAYER:

Jesus, of all the voices in the world, I want to hear yours the clearest. Help me to grow to recognize your voice and know it well. Help me to think about what's true and lovely and good. I want to follow your voice all the days of my life.

ENTHUSIASM

Work with enthusiasm, as though you were working for the Lord rather than for people.

Ephesians 6:7 nlt

Sometimes God gives a person wealth and possessions. God makes it possible for that person to enjoy them. God helps them accept the life he has given them. God helps them to be happy in their work. All these things are gifts from God.

Ecclesiastes 5:19 nirv

By You I can run against a troop,
By my God I can leap over a wall.

Psalm 18:29 nkjv

Whatever your hand finds to do,
do it with all your might.

Ecclesiastes 9:10 niv

66

Everything else is worthless when compared with the priceless gain of knowing Christ Jesus my Lord. I have put aside all else, counting it worth less than nothing, in order that I can have Christ.... Now I have given up everything else—I have found it to be the only way to really know Christ and to experience the mighty power that brought him back to life again, and to find out what it means to suffer and to die with him. So whatever it takes, I will be one who lives in the fresh newness of life of those who are alive from the dead.

PHILIPPIANS 3:8,10-11 TLB

EQUIPPING

All scripture is inspired by God and is useful for teaching, for reproof, for correction, and for training in righteousness, so that everyone who belongs to God may be proficient, equipped for every good work.

2 TIMOTHY 3:16–17 NRSV

May He give you the power to accomplish all the good things your faith prompts you to do.

2 THESSALONIANS 1:11 NLT

Then the LORD reached out his hand and touched my mouth and said to me, "I have put my words in your mouth."

JEREMIAH 1:9 NIV

We are God's handiwork, created in Christ Jesus to do good works, which God prepared in advance for us to do.

EPHESIANS 2:10 NIV

So then, my beloved, just as you have always obeyed, not as in my presence only, but now much more in my absence, work out your salvation with fear and trembling; for it is God who is at work in you, both to will and to work for His good pleasure.

PHILIPPIANS 2:12-13 NASB

If any of you lacks wisdom, you should ask God, who gives generously to all without finding fault, and it will be given to you.

JAMES 1:5 NIV

ETERNITY

We fix our eyes not on what is seen, but on what is unseen, since what is seen is temporary, but what is unseen is eternal.

2 CORINTHIANS 4:18 NIV

Before the mountains were brought forth,
or ever you had formed the earth and the world,
from everlasting to everlasting you are God.

PSALM 90:2 ESV

I'm asking the LORD for only one thing.
Here is what I want.
I want to live in the house of the LORD
all the days of my life.
I want to look at the beauty of the LORD.
I want to worship him in his temple.

PSALM 27:4 NIRV

Surely goodness and mercy shall follow me All the days of my life; And I will dwell in the house of the LORD Forever.

PSALM 23:6 NKJV

We are citizens of heaven, where the Lord Jesus Christ lives. And we are eagerly waiting for him to return as our Savior. He will take our weak mortal bodies and change them into glorious bodies like his own, using the same power with which he will bring everything under his control.

PHILIPPIANS 3:20–21 NLT

"I will come back and take you to be with me that you also may be where I am."

JOHN 14:3 NIV

FAITH

Faith is confidence in what we hope for and
assurance about what we do not see.

HEBREWS 11:1 NIV

"Not one word of all the good words which the LORD
your God spoke concerning you has failed; all have
been fulfilled for you, not one of them has failed."

JOSHUA 23:14 NASB

As we pray to our God and Father about you, we
think of your faithful work, your loving deeds, and
the enduring hope you have because of our Lord
Jesus Christ.

1 THESSALONIANS 1:3 NLT

Faith comes by hearing,
and hearing by the word of God.

ROMANS 10:17 NKJV

"If you have faith like a grain of mustard seed, you will say to this mountain, 'Move from here to there,' and it will move, and nothing will be impossible for you."

MATTHEW 17:20 ESV

Through Christ you have come to trust in God. And you have placed your faith and hope in God because he raised Christ from the dead and gave him great glory.

1 PETER 1:21 NLT

"Until heaven and earth disappear, not the smallest letter, not the least stroke of a pen, will by any means disappear from the Law until everything is accomplished."

MATTHEW 5:18 NIV

"If you sinful people know how to give good gifts to your children, how much more will your heavenly Father give good gifts to those who ask him."

MATTHEW 7:11 NLT

Infants rely completely and utterly on their parents for survival. They are born trusting that they will be held, fed, and kept warm and safe. As they get older, though, they become more independent.

As you become an adult, you may naturally feel as if you need your parents less. Still, there are huge questions about the future looming: Where am I going to college? Where am I going to live? How am I going to be able to provide for myself? The future can seem daunting as you try to figure out how to set out on your own.

Even though you outgrow your need for complete dependence on a parent, you never outgrow your need for God. You don't have to have all the answers to your future. You can take comfort in knowing that God is a faithful God, he loves you, and he will provide for every need.

PRAYER:

Jesus, as I get older, I pray I'd never grow away from you. I don't want to fear the future but trust in your tender care. I know I can depend on you for everything I need.

FEAR

Where God's love is, there is no fear, because God's perfect love drives out fear. It is punishment that makes a person fear, so love is not made perfect in the person who fears.

1 John 4:18 NCV

Don't be afraid, for I am with you.
Don't be discouraged, for I am your God.
I will strengthen you and help you.
I will hold you up with my victorious right hand.

Isaiah 41:10 NLT

The Lord is my light and my salvation;
whom shall I fear?
The Lord is the stronghold of my life;
of whom shall I be afraid?

Psalm 27:1 ESV

God has not given us a spirit of fear,
but of power and of love and of a sound mind.

2 TIMOTHY 1:7 NKJV

Say to those with fearful hearts,
"Be strong, and do not fear,
for your God...is coming to save you."

ISAIAH 35:4 NLT

When you lie down, you will not be afraid;
when you lie down, your sleep will be sweet.
Have no fear of sudden disaster
or of the ruin that overtakes the wicked,
for the LORD will be at your side
and will keep your foot from being snared.

PROVERBS 3:24–26 NIV

FORGIVENESS

You, Lord, are good, and ready to forgive,
And abundant in mercy to all those
who call upon You.

PSALM 86:5 NKJV

"Whenever you stand praying, forgive, if you have
anything against anyone, so that your Father also
who is in heaven may forgive you."

MARK 11:25 ESV

As far as the east is from the west,
So far has He removed our transgressions from us.

PSALM 103:12 NASB

If we confess our sins, He is faithful and just to
forgive us our sins and to cleanse us from all
unrighteousness.

1 JOHN 1:9 NKJV

He is so rich in kindness and grace that he
purchased our freedom with the blood of his
Son and forgave our sins.

EPHESIANS 1:7 NLT

My sacrifice, O God, is a broken spirit;
a broken and contrite heart
you, God, will not despise.

PSALM 51:17 NIV

"Her sins—and they are many—have been forgiven,
so she has shown me much love. But a person
who is forgiven little shows only little love."

LUKE 7:47 NLT

"If you forgive other people when they sin against
you, your heavenly Father will also forgive you."

MATTHEW 6:14 NIV

FREEDOM

Now that you have been set free from sin and have become slaves of God, the benefit you reap leads to holiness, and the result is eternal life.

ROMANS 6:22 NIV

"If you hold to my teaching, you are really my disciples. Then you will know the truth, and the truth will set you free."

JOHN 8:31–32 NIV

So Christ has truly set us free. Now make sure that you stay free, and don't get tied up again in slavery to the law.

GALATIANS 5:1 NLT

He has delivered us from the power of darkness and conveyed us into the kingdom of the Son of His love.

COLOSSIANS 1:13 NKJV

There is now no condemnation for those who are in Christ Jesus, because through Christ Jesus the law of the Spirit who gives life has set you free from the law of sin and death.

ROMANS 8:1-2 NIV

Understand what we are telling you: You can have forgiveness of your sins through Jesus. The law of Moses could not free you from your sins. But through Jesus everyone who believes is free from all sins.

ACTS 13:38-39 NCV

Now the Lord is the Spirit, and where the Spirit of the Lord is, there is freedom.

2 CORINTHIANS 3:17 NRSV

Don't let the excitement of youth cause you to forget your Creator. Honor him in your youth before you grow old and say, "Life is not pleasant anymore." Remember him before the light of the sun, moon, and stars is dim to your old eyes, and rain clouds continually darken your sky.

ECCLESIASTES 12:1-2 NLT

Managing school loans, rent, and a brand new job full of responsibilities can feel exhausting. Each day brings a set of problems to solve and expectations to meet.

In the middle of a busy season, it is easy to feel like we are alone, that no one can possibly understand the strain and stress we are under. We want to live life well for God, but at the end of the day we feel drained with nothing else to give.

There is only so much we can handle in one day. God understands that. But he asks us to put him first. When that priority is set, the others fall into place. As we do other things throughout our day, he'll renew and refresh us. When we feel depleted, he supports us.

PRAYER:

God, thank you that when life seems like too much, you are there to help me face another day. Remind me to put you first and depend more on you and less on my abilities and strength. I want to remember you each day and be excited by all that you are doing in my life even when it's difficult to see.

FRIENDSHIP

The LORD is near to all who call on him,
to all who call on him in truth.

PSALM 145:18 NIV

"Here I am! I stand at the door and knock. If anyone
hears my voice and opens the door, I will come in
and eat with that person, and they with me."

REVELATION 3:20 NIV

Turn to me and have mercy,
for I am alone and in deep distress.

PSALM 25:16 NLT

A wise warning to someone who will listen
is as valuable as gold earrings or fine gold jewelry.
Trustworthy messengers refresh those who send them,
like the coolness of snow in the summertime.

PROVERBS 25:12–13 NCV

By this we know that we abide in Him and He in us, because He has given us of His Spirit.

1 JOHN 4:13 NASB

A friend loves at all times.

PROVERBS 17:17 NKJV

"Behold, I am with you always,
to the end of the age."

MATTHEW 28:20 ESV

GENEROSITY

Let each one give as he purposes in his heart,
not grudgingly or of necessity;
for God loves a cheerful giver.

2 CORINTHIANS 9:7 NKJV

It is more blessed to give than to receive.

ACTS 20:35 NIV

One man gives freely, yet gains even more;
another withholds unduly, but comes to poverty.
A generous man will prosper;
whoever refreshes others will be refreshed.

PROVERBS 11:24–25 NIV

Whoever is generous to the poor lends to the Lord,
and he will repay him for his deed.

PROVERBS 19:17 ESV

"When you give to the needy, do not let your left hand know what your right hand is doing, so that your giving may be in secret. Then your Father, who sees what is done in secret, will reward you."

MATTHEW 6:3–4 NIV

You shall generously give to him, and your heart shall not be grieved when you give to him, because for this thing the Lord your God will bless you in all your work and in all your undertakings.

DEUTERONOMY 15:10 NASB

The generous will themselves be blessed, for they share their food with the poor.

PROVERBS 22:9 NIV

GENTLENESS

A gentle answer deflects anger,
but harsh words make tempers flare.

PROVERBS 15:1 NLT

Remind the believers to yield to the authority of rulers
and government leaders, to obey them, to be ready
to do good, to speak no evil about anyone, to live in
peace, and to be gentle and polite to all people.

TITUS 3:1-2 NCV

The wisdom that comes from heaven is first of all
pure and full of quiet gentleness. Then it is peace-
loving and courteous. It allows discussion and is
willing to yield to others; it is full of mercy and
good deeds. It is wholehearted and straightforward
and sincere.

JAMES 3:17 TLB

In your hearts revere Christ as Lord. Always be prepared to give an answer to everyone who asks you to give the reason for the hope that you have. But do this with gentleness and respect.

1 PETER 3:15 NIV

"Blessed are the gentle,
for they shall inherit the earth."

MATTHEW 5:5 NASB

Let your gentleness be evident to all.
The Lord is near.

PHILIPPIANS 4:5 NIV

You have given me the shield of your salvation,
and your right hand supported me,
and your gentleness made me great.

PSALM 18:35 ESV

GRACE

Where is another God like you,
who pardons the sins
of the survivors among his people?
You cannot stay angry with your people,
for you love to be merciful.
Once again you will have compassion on us.
You will tread our sins beneath your feet;
you will throw them into
the depths of the ocean!
You will bless us as you
promised Jacob long ago.
You will set your love upon us,
as you promised our father Abraham!

MICAH 7:18–20 TLB

Sin shall no longer be your master,
because you are not under the law, but under grace.

ROMANS 6:14 NIV

He gives more grace. Therefore He says:
"God resists the proud,
But gives grace to the humble."

JAMES 4:6 NKJV

God is so rich in mercy, and he loved us so much, that even though we were dead because of our sins, he gave us life when he raised Christ from the dead. (It is only by God's grace that you have been saved!)... God saved you by his grace when you believed. And you can't take credit for this; it is a gift from God. Salvation is not a reward for the good things we have done, so none of us can boast about it.

EPHESIANS 2:4–5, 8–9 NLT

You do not know what will happen tomorrow! Your life is like a mist. You can see it for a short time, but then it goes away.

JAMES 4:14 NCV

Sometimes it feels like life is spinning around you. You wish you could just catch it in your hand and hold on to it for a moment, long enough to take a good look.

We do our best to plan, but in many ways life is an unpredictable adventure. It takes what you are and shapes who you become. It is both the platform to succeed as well as the beautiful chance to make mistakes and learn.

In the end, our life is short. It's like a mist that settles thick in the early morning but evaporates in the morning sun. In the context of eternity, it's the blink of an eye. So make it count. Do something with your life that will outlive you. Don't focus on joining the rat race. Focus on changing the world—and make a change that will last long after you've made it.

PRAYER:

God, my life is everything to me, but it shouldn't be. You should be everything to me because you are the only one who can take my temporary life and make an eternal impact out of it. Lead me to live in a way that makes a difference.

GRATITUDE

That my soul may sing praise to You
and not be silent.
O Lord my God, I will give thanks to You forever.

Psalm 30:12 NASB

Thanks be to God for his indescribable gift!

2 Corinthians 9:15 NIV

Be filled with the Holy Spirit, singing psalms and
hymns and spiritual songs among yourselves, and
making music to the Lord in your hearts. And give
thanks for everything to God the Father in the name
of our Lord Jesus Christ.

Ephesians 5:18–20 NLT

Give thanks to the Lord, for he is good.
His love endures forever.

Psalm 136:1 NIV

Always be thankful. Let the message about Christ, in all its richness, fill your lives. Teach and counsel each other with all the wisdom he gives. Sing psalms and hymns and spiritual songs to God with thankful hearts. And whatever you do or say, do it as a representative of the Lord Jesus, giving thanks through him to God the Father.

COLOSSIANS 3:15-17 NLT

In everything give thanks;
for this is God's will for you in Christ Jesus.

1 THESSALONIANS 5:18 NASB

Now therefore, our God,
We thank You And praise Your glorious name.

1 CHRONICLES 29:13 NKJV

GUIDANCE

Whether you turn to the right or to the left,
your ears will hear a voice behind you, saying,
"This is the way; walk in it."

ISAIAH 30:21 NIV

We can make our plans,
but the LORD determines our steps.

PROVERBS 16:9 NLT

Guide me in your truth and teach me,
for you are God my Savior,
and my hope is in you all day long.

PSALM 25:5 NIV

The true children of God are those who let God's
Spirit lead them.

ROMANS 8:14 NCV

Trust in the Lord with all your heart,

And lean not on your own understanding;

In all your ways acknowledge Him,

And He shall direct your paths.

PROVERBS 3:5-6 NKJV

We ask God to give you complete knowledge of his will and to give you spiritual wisdom and understanding. Then the way you live will always honor and please the Lord, and your lives will produce every kind of good fruit. All the while, you will grow as you learn to know God better and better.

COLOSSIANS 1:9-10 NLT

Listen to advice and accept discipline,

and at the end you will be counted among the wise.

PROVERBS 19:20 NIV

HAPPINESS

Happy are those who hear the joyful call to worship,
for they will walk in the light of your presence, Lord.

PSALM 89:15 NLT

May you be filled with joy, always thanking the
Father. He has enabled you to share in the inheritance
that belongs to his people, who live in the light.

COLOSSIANS 1:11–12 NLT

Enter his gates with thanksgiving,
and his courts with praise.
Give thanks to him, bless his name.
For the Lord is good;
his steadfast love endures forever,
and his faithfulness to all generations.

PSALM 100:4–5 NRSV

"He will yet fill your mouth with laughter
and your lips with shouts of joy."

JOB 8:21 NIV

The Lord has done great things for us,
and we are filled with joy.

PSALM 126:3 NIV

I know that there is nothing better for people
than to be happy and to do good while they live.

ECCLESIASTES 3:12 NIV

I will give thanks to the LORD with my whole heart;
I will recount all of your wonderful deeds.
I will be glad and exult in you;
I will sing praise to your name, O Most High.

PSALM 9:1-2 ESV

Sensible people keep their eyes glued on wisdom,
but a fool's eyes wander to the ends of the earth.

PROVERBS 17:24 NLT

What is it about our hearts that makes them prone
to wander? We love the Lord deeply and we want to
follow him, but there are so many things that lead
us away. Life after graduation can be the time when
that happens most. There are so many things that
tempt our hearts.

These years can be difficult, but they can also be
some of the best! Stay strong. Remember that you
are God's child, and he knows you by name. He's
jealous for your heart; he doesn't want to share you
with anything or anyone else that would harm you.

Hold fast to God's love. Don't allow the things in this world to make you wander. Be one of the few who chooses to keep their eyes glued on wisdom, and spend every moment you can living your best in his love.

PRAYER:

God, help me to never wander from you. I know that nothing this world has to offer will ever bring me as much joy as you do. Show me the things I should say yes to and things I should refuse. I trust in your faithfulness and goodness to me.

HEALING

Trust the LORD with all your heart,
and don't depend on your own understanding.
Remember the LORD in all you do,
and he will give you success.
Don't depend on your own wisdom.
Respect the LORD and refuse to do wrong.
Then your body will be healthy,
and your bones will be strong.

PROVERBS 3:5–8 NCV

He was pierced for our transgressions,
he was crushed for our iniquities;
the punishment that brought us peace was on him,
and by his wounds we are healed.

ISAIAH 53:5 NIV

A cheerful heart does good like medicine.

PROVERBS 17:22 TLB

"Daughter, your faith has made you well;
go in peace and be healed of your affliction."

MARK 5:34 NASB

My child, pay attention to what I say.
Listen carefully to my words.
Don't lose sight of them.
Let them penetrate deep into your heart,
for they bring life to those who find them,
and healing to their whole body.

PROVERBS 4:20–22 NLT

The world and its desires pass away,
but whoever does the will of God lives forever.

1 JOHN 2:17 NIV

HONESTY

Those who deal truthfully are His delight.

PROVERBS 12:22 NKJV

Putting away falsehood,
let all of us speak the truth to our neighbors,
for we are members of one another.

EPHESIANS 4:25 NRSV

Who may stand before the Lord? Only those
with pure hands and hearts, who do not practice
dishonesty and lying. They will receive God's own
goodness as their blessing from him.

PSALM 24:4 TLB

"I always try to do what I believe is right before God
and people."

ACTS 24:16 NCV

Speaking the truth in love, we will grow to become in every respect the mature body of him who is the head, that is, Christ.

EPHESIANS 4:15 NIV

Who may worship in your sanctuary, LORD?
Who may enter your presence on your holy hill?
Those who lead blameless lives and do what is right,
speaking the truth from sincere hearts.

PSALM 15:1-2 NLT

"Nothing is hidden that will not be made manifest, nor is anything secret that will not be known and come to light."

LUKE 8:17 ESV

HOPE

The LORD raises the poor up from the dust,
and he lifts the needy from the ashes.
He lets the poor sit with princes
and receive a throne of honor.

1 SAMUEL 2:8 NCV

Blessed be the God and Father of our Lord Jesus
Christ! According to his great mercy, he has caused
us to be born again to a living hope through the
resurrection of Jesus Christ.

1 PETER 1:3 ESV

May the God of hope fill you with all joy and peace
as you trust in him, so that you may overflow with
hope by the power of the Holy Spirit.

ROMANS 15:13 NIV

The LORD is good to those whose hope is in him,
to the one who seeks him.

LAMENTATIONS 3:25 NIV

There is surely a future hope for you,
and your hope will not be cut off.

PROVERBS 23:18 NIV

We can rejoice, too, when we run into problems
and trials, for we know that they help us
develop endurance. And endurance develops
strength of character, and character strengthens
our confident hope of salvation. And this hope
will not lead to disappointment. For we know how
dearly God loves us, because he has given us the
Holy Spirit to fill our hearts with his love.

ROMANS 5:3–5 NLT

HUMILITY

Humility is the fear of the Lord;
its wages are riches and honor and life.

PROVERBS 22:4 NIV

Where you have envy and selfish ambition, there
you find disorder and every evil practice. But the
wisdom that comes from heaven is first of all pure;
then peace-loving, considerate, submissive, full
of mercy and good fruit, impartial and sincere.
Peacemakers who sow in peace reap a harvest of
righteousness.

JAMES 3:16–18 NIV

Those who accept correction gain understanding.
Respect for the Lord will teach you wisdom.
If you want to be honored, you must be humble.

PROVERBS 15:32–33 NCV

In your relationships with one another,
have the same mindset as Christ Jesus:
Who, being in very nature God,
did not consider equality with God something
to be used to his own advantage;
rather, he made himself nothing
by taking the very nature of a servant,
being made in human likeness.
And being found in appearance as a man,
he humbled himself
by becoming obedient to death—
even death on a cross!
Therefore God exalted him to the highest place
and gave him the name that is above every name.

PHILIPPIANS 2:5–9 NIV

I cried out, "I am slipping!"
but your unfailing love, O Lord, supported me.
When doubts filled my mind,
your comfort gave me renewed hope and cheer.

ISAIAH 94:18-19 NLT

Life is full of ups and downs, victories and failures. Many times we feel great, and life is going well. Then there are moments when our foot slips, and we find ourselves losing our balance. Sometimes we're on top of the world; other times we're ready to give up. We don't always feel strong.

It may seem like God is more present when things are going well. But even at our lowest, God is there. His love is unfailing, and it will support us through the darkest times.

Don't be afraid of your own doubts. God is big enough to renew your hope and to restore your faith. He will walk with you through the darkest times and rejoice with you through the greatest.

PRAYER:

Thank you, God, for being there for me always—when things are at their best and things are at their worst. When sadness comes over me, bring me joy. When worry takes over my mind, give me hope and peace. When I'm happy, join me in celebrating.

INSPIRATION

The precepts of the LORD are right,
giving joy to the heart.
The commands of the LORD are radiant,
giving light to the eyes.

PSALM 19:8 NIV

"I am the Light of the world;
he who follows Me will not walk in the darkness,
but will have the Light of life."

JOHN 8:12 NASB

Live in the right way, serve God, have faith, love,
patience, and gentleness. Fight the good fight
of faith, grabbing hold of the life that continues
forever. You were called to have that life when
you confessed the good confession before many
witnesses.

1 TIMOTHY 6:11–12 NCV

Your laws are my treasure;
they are my heart's delight.

PSALM 119:111 NLT

I have been crucified with Christ; and it is no longer I who live, but Christ lives in me.

GALATIANS 2:20 NASB

"You are the light of the world. A city set on a hill cannot be hidden. Nor do people light a lamp and put it under a basket, but on a stand, and it gives light to all in the house. In the same way, let your light shine before others, so that they may see your good works and give glory to your Father who is in heaven."

MATTHEW 5:14–16 ESV

JOY

Satisfy us in the morning with your unfailing love,
that we may sing for joy and be glad all our days.

PSALM 90:14 NIV

Be truly glad. There is wonderful joy ahead. You love
him even though you have never seen him. Though
you do not see him now, you trust him; and you
rejoice with a glorious, inexpressible joy.

1 PETER 1:6, 8 NLT

Our mouth was filled with laughter,
and our tongue with shouts of joy.

PSALM 126:2 ESV

"Until now you have not asked for anything
in my name. Ask and you will receive,
and your joy will be complete."

JOHN 16:24 NIV

Let all those rejoice who put their trust in You;
Let them ever shout for joy,
because You defend them;
Let those also who love Your name
Be joyful in You.

PSALM 5:11 NKJV

"I have told you this so that my joy may be in you
and that your joy may be complete."

JOHN 15:11 NIV

You will go out in joy
and be led forth in peace;
the mountains and hills
will burst into song before you,
and all the trees of the field
will clap their hands.

ISAIAH 55:12 NIV

JUSTICE

Do not avenge yourselves, but rather give place to wrath; for it is written, "Vengeance is Mine, I will repay," says the Lord.

ROMANS 12:19 NKJV

He will not break the bruised reed, nor quench the dimly burning flame. He will encourage the fainthearted, those tempted to despair. He will see full justice given to all who have been wronged.

ISAIAH 42:3 TLB

The LORD secures justice for the poor and upholds the cause of the needy.

PSALM 140:12 NIV

Righteousness and justice are the foundation of Your throne.

PSALM 89:14 NKJV

He will not judge by appearance, false evidence, or hearsay, but will defend the poor and the exploited. He will rule against the wicked who oppress them. For he will be clothed with fairness and with truth.

ISAIAH 11:3–5 TLB

He did not retaliate when he was insulted,
nor threaten revenge when he suffered.
He left his case in the hands of God,
who always judges fairly.

1 PETER 2:23 NLT

LORD, you know the hopes of the helpless. Surely you will hear their cries and comfort them. You will bring justice to the orphans and the oppressed, so mere people can no longer terrify them.

PSALM 10:17–18 NLT

How much better to get wisdom than gold,
to get insight rather than silver!
The highway of the upright avoids evil;
Those who guard their ways preserve their lives.

PROVERBS 16:16-17 NIV

It's all about the money, right? Most of us place a lot of value on being financially successful. After all, money is what gets us pretty much everything we want. We focus on our education, so we can get a good job, so we can make a good wage, so we can buy what we want.

But the Bible clearly tells us that it's more important to be wise than to be rich. You can have all the money in the world and be a fool.

Money might take you all the way on this earth, but it won't take you anywhere in eternity. When you die, you can't take money with you. What matters is the life you led, the people you impacted, and the glory you gave to God. Those are the things that last into eternity. Strive to achieve success in the things that matter!

PRAYER:

God, help me to pursue wisdom above treasure, and insight above success. Give me eternal vision that will help me to choose based on what will last instead of what will fade. I want to guard my way and live for things that matter in eternity.

LIFE

My child, pay attention to my words;
listen closely to what I say.
Don't ever forget my words;
keep them always in mind.
They are the key to life for those who find them;
they bring health to the whole body.
Be careful what you think,
because your thoughts run your life.

PROVERBS 4:20–23 NCV

"I am the resurrection and the life. He who believes
in Me, though he may die, he shall live."

JOHN 11:25 NKJV

"I am the Light of the world; he who follows Me
will not walk in the darkness, but will have the
Light of life."

JOHN 8:12 NASB

The law came to make sin worse. But when sin grew worse, God's grace increased. Sin once used death to rule us, but God gave people more of his grace so that grace could rule by making people right with him. And this brings life forever through Jesus Christ our Lord.

ROMANS 5:20–21 NCV

We don't give up. Our bodies are becoming weaker and weaker. But our spirits are being renewed day by day. Our troubles are small. They last only for a short time. But they are earning for us a glory that will last forever. It is greater than all our troubles.

2 CORINTHIANS 4:16-17 NIRV

LOVE

The steadfast love of the LORD never ceases;
his mercies never come to an end;
they are new every morning;
great is your faithfulness.

LAMENTATIONS 3:22–23 ESV

Know therefore that the LORD your God is God;
he is the faithful God, keeping his covenant of love
to a thousand generations of those who love him
and keep his commandments.

DEUTERONOMY 7:9 NIV

Let love and faithfulness never leave you;
bind them around your neck,
write them on the tablet of your heart.

PROVERBS 3:3 NIV

We have come to know and have believed the love which God has for us. God is love, and the one who abides in love abides in God, and God abides in him. We love, because He first loved us.

1 JOHN 4:16, 19 NASB

Three things will last forever—faith, hope, and love—and the greatest of these is love.

1 CORINTHIANS 13:13 NLT

I will sing of the LORD's great love forever; with my mouth I will make your faithfulness known through all generations. I will declare that your love stands firm forever, that you have established your faithfulness in heaven itself.

PSALM 89:1–2 NIV

PATIENCE

The LORD longs to be gracious to you;
therefore he will rise up to show you compassion.
For the LORD is a God of justice.
Blessed are all who wait for him!

ISAIAH 30:18 NIV

The Lord isn't really being slow about his promise,
as some people think. No, he is being patient
for your sake. He does not want anyone to be
destroyed, but wants everyone to repent.

2 PETER 3:9 NLT

As a prisoner for the Lord, then, I urge you to
live a life worthy of the calling you have received.
Be completely humble and gentle; be patient,
bearing with one another in love.

EPHESIANS 4:1-2 NIV

"They are those who, hearing the word,
hold it fast in an honest and good heart,
and bear fruit with patience."

LUKE 8:15 ESV

We are saved by trusting. And trusting means
looking forward to getting something we don't
yet have—for a man who already has something
doesn't need to hope and trust that he will get it.
But if we must keep trusting God for something
that hasn't happened yet, it teaches us to wait
patiently and confidently.

ROMANS 8:24-25 TLB

Imitate those who through faith and patience
inherit what has been promised.

HEBREWS 6:12 NIV

PEACE

"These things I have spoken to you, so that in Me you may have peace. In the world you have tribulation, but take courage; I have overcome the world."

JOHN 16:33 NASB

The LORD will give strength to His people;
The LORD will bless His people with peace.

PSALM 29:11 NKJV

"Peace I leave with you; my peace I give you.
I do not give to you as the world gives. Do not let your hearts be troubled and do not be afraid."

JOHN 14:27 NIV

If people's thinking is controlled by the sinful self, there is death. But if their thinking is controlled by the Spirit, there is life and peace.

ROMANS 8:6 NCV

Those who love your instructions have great peace and do not stumble.

PSALM 119:165 NLT

God is not a God of confusion but of peace.

1 CORINTHIANS 14:33 NASB

Let the peace of Christ rule in your hearts, since as members of one body you were called to peace.

COLOSSIANS 3:15 NIV

May the Lord of peace himself give you peace at all times and in every way. The Lord be with all of you.

2 THESSALONIANS 3:16 NIV

"Return to your home, and declare how much God has done for you." So he went away, proclaiming throughout the city how much Jesus had done for him.

LUKE 8:39 NRSV

No experience in your life is wasted. God always has something he can teach you. You may not even understand until years later why God brought you through something specific. But someday, it will all make sense.

Sometimes God will teach you things for your own growth. Other times it's not about you at all. Sometimes God will lead you through experiences or show you things so you can impact someone's life with your story.

Don't ever think that your story isn't good enough or interesting enough or happy enough or dramatic enough. Your story is your story— no one else has one the same—and it will help someone in a way that nothing else could. Share your life story with others, and bring them encouragement today.

PRAYER:

Heavenly Father, sometimes I don't understand why certain things happen to me. I don't know why my life looks the way that it does. But I trust that you have a unique plan for me that couldn't be lived out by anyone else. Help me trust in your purposes.

PERSEVERANCE

God blesses those who patiently endure testing and temptation. Afterward they will receive the crown of life that God has promised to those who love him.

JAMES 1:12 NLT

Let us not grow weary of doing good,
for in due season we will reap, if we do not give up.

GALATIANS 6:9 ESV

Wait on the LORD;
Be of good courage,
And He shall strengthen your heart;
Wait, I say, on the LORD!

PSALM 27:14 NKJV

May the Lord direct your hearts into God's love and Christ's perseverance.

2 THESSALONIANS 3:5 NIV

"The one who endures to the end will be saved."

MATTHEW 24:13 ESV

Consider it pure joy...whenever you face trials of many kinds, because you know that the testing of your faith develops perseverance. Let perseverance finish its work so that you may be mature and complete, not lacking anything.

JAMES 1:2–4 NIV

Since we are surrounded by such a great cloud of witnesses, let us throw off everything that hinders and the sin that so easily entangles. And let us run with perseverance the race marked out for us, fixing our eyes on Jesus. ...so that you will not grow weary and lose heart.

HEBREWS 12:1–3 NIV

PRAYER

My voice You shall hear in the morning, O Lord;
In the morning I will direct it to You,
And I will look up.

PSALM 5:3 NKJV

"Ask and it will be given to you; seek and you will
find; knock and the door will be opened to you.
For everyone who asks receives; he who seeks finds;
and to him who knocks, the door will be opened."

MATTHEW 7:7–8 NIV

I call on you, My God, for you will answer me;
turn your ear to me and hear my prayer.

PSALM 17:6 NIV

The prayer of a righteous person is powerful and
effective.

JAMES 5:16 NIV

The Spirit also helps our weakness; for we do not know how to pray as we should, but the Spirit Himself intercedes for us with groanings too deep for words.

ROMANS 8:26 NASB

Pray without ceasing.

1 THESSALONIANS 5:17 NKJV

You, God, are my God,
earnestly I seek you;
I thirst for you,
my whole being longs for you,
in a dry and parched land
where there is no water.

PSALM 63:1 NIV

PROTECTION

The LORD himself goes before you
and will be with you;
he will never leave you nor forsake you.

DEUTERONOMY 31:8 NIV

If you make the LORD your refuge,
if you make the Most High your shelter,
no evil will conquer you;
no plague will come near your home.
For he will order his angels
to protect you wherever you go.

PSALM 91:9–11 NLT

How great is the goodness you have stored up for
those who fear you. You lavish it on those who
come to you for protection, blessing them before
the watching world.

PSALM 31:19 NLT

The Lord is faithful, and he will strengthen you
and protect you.

2 THESSALONIANS 3:3 NIV

The LORD will keep you from all harm—
he will watch over your life;
the LORD will watch over your coming and going
both now and forevermore.

PSALM 121:7–8 NIV

Let all who take refuge in you be glad;
let them ever sing for joy.
Spread your protection over them,
that those who love your name may rejoice in you.

PSALM 5:11 NIV

WORKING FOR THE LORD

Whatever you do, work at it with all your heart, as working for the Lord, not for human masters, since you know that you will receive an inheritance from the Lord as a reward. It is the Lord Christ you are serving.

COLOSSIANS 3:23-24 NIV

We all have those moments when we feel like our job is awful or that life is boring. But if we stop and consider this verse, we learn that it is important to treat our work and responsibilities as if we were there for God.

Work harder than the person next to you. Strive to excel in everything. Go the extra mile and do more than what is expected of you.

The next time that you're feeling underappreciated, bored, or tired of your work—use those feelings as motivation to work even harder. Remember that as a Christian, the world is constantly examining you to see what kind of person you really are. By striving to be excellent at what you do, you'll bring praise to God.

PRAYER:

Lord, help me remember that I am your representative. I want people to speak well of me because I serve you. I really want others to know that I work hard and strive for excellence because I know that I am doing it for you.

PURITY

Our faces, then, are not covered. We all show the Lord's glory, and we are being changed to be like him. This change in us brings ever greater glory, which comes from the Lord, who is the Spirit.

2 Corinthians 3:18 NCV

Teach me your ways, O Lord,
that I may live according to your truth!
Grant me purity of heart,
so that I may honor you.

Psalm 86:11 NLT

Whatever is true, whatever is honorable, whatever is just, whatever is pure, whatever is lovely, whatever is commendable, if there is any excellence, if there is anything worthy of praise, think about these things.

Philippians 4:8 ESV

Now that you have purified yourselves by obeying the truth so that you have sincere love for each other, love one another deeply, from the heart.

1 PETER 1:22 NIV

Examine everything carefully; hold fast to that which is good; abstain from every form of evil.

1 THESSALONIANS 5:21-22 NASB

Do everything without grumbling or arguing, so that you may become blameless and pure, "children of God without fault in a warped and crooked generation." Then you will shine among them like stars in the sky as you hold firmly to the word of life.

PHILIPPIANS 2:14-16 NIV

PURPOSE

God's solid foundation stands firm, sealed with this inscription: "The Lord knows those who are his."

2 TIMOTHY 2:19 NIV

When I was a child, I spoke and thought and reasoned as a child. But when I grew up, I put away childish things. Now we see things imperfectly, like puzzling reflections in a mirror, but then we will see everything with perfect clarity. All that I know now is partial and incomplete, but then I will know everything completely, just as God now knows me completely.

1 CORINTHIANS 13:11–12 NLT

"For I know the plans I have for you,"
declares the LORD,
"plans to prosper you and not to harm you,
plans to give you hope and a future."

JEREMIAH 29:11 NIV

I will instruct you and teach you
in the way you should go;
I will counsel you with my loving eye on you.

PSALM 32:8 NIV

O Lord, You have searched me and known me.
You know my sitting down and my rising up;
You understand my thought afar off.
You comprehend my path and my lying down,
And are acquainted with all my ways.
For there is not a word on my tongue,
But behold, O Lord, You know it altogether.

PSALM 139:1–4 NKJV

RECONCILIATION

You were separate from Christ...foreigners to the covenants of the promise, without hope and without God in the world. But now in Christ Jesus you who once were far away have been brought near by the blood of Christ.

EPHESIANS 2:12–13 NIV

We are made right with God by placing our faith in Jesus Christ. And this is true for everyone who believes, no matter who we are. For everyone has sinned; we all fall short of God's glorious standard. Yet God, with undeserved kindness, declares that we are righteous. He did this through Christ Jesus when he freed us from the penalty for our sins.

ROMANS 3:22–24 NLT

We have stopped evaluating others from a human point of view. At one time we thought of Christ merely from a human point of view. How differently we know him now! This means that anyone who belongs to Christ has become a new person. The old life is gone; a new life has begun! And all of this is a gift from God, who brought us back to himself through Christ. And God has given us this task of reconciling people to him.

2 CORINTHIANS 5:16–18 NLT

REDEMPTION

We have been made right with God because of our faith. Now we have peace with him because of our Lord Jesus Christ. Through faith in Jesus we have received God's grace. In that grace we stand. We are full of joy because we expect to share in God's glory.

ROMANS 5:1–2 NIRV

Once you were dead because of your disobedience and your many sins. All of us used to live that way, following the passionate desires and inclinations of our sinful nature. By our very nature we were subject to God's anger, just like everyone else. But God is so rich in mercy, and he loved us so much, that even though we were dead because of our sins, he gave us life when he raised Christ from the dead.

EPHESIANS 2:1, 3–5 NLT

Be gracious to me, O God,
according to Your lovingkindness;
According to the greatness of Your compassion
blot out my transgressions.

PSALM 51:1 NASB

UNLESS THE LORD

Unless the LORD builds the house,
the builders labor in vain.
Unless the LORD watches over the city,
the guards stand watch in vain.

PSALM 127:1 NIV

Don't try to fight for something that God isn't in.
Sometimes it's tempting to start something, and
then ask God to bless it after the fact. But did he
really want you to start it? If you take a job without
seeking God, you need to find out if that job is
God's will for you *before* you ask him to bless it.

Seek the face of the Lord continually. He will speak
into your life and will guide and direct you if you
have opened your heart to him.

When you are walking in continual communication with God, your life will reflect his blessing and his peace. Only he knows the end from the beginning—so why wouldn't you trust your life to him?

PRAYER:

God, I don't want to build something in my life that you're not a part of. I don't want to start something if your blessing isn't on it. Guide me in all things so I can put myself fully into the things that you've ordained.

REFRESHMENT

The law of the LORD is perfect,
refreshing the soul.
The statutes of the LORD are trustworthy,
making wise the simple.

PSALM 19:7 NIV

Your love, LORD, reaches to the heavens,
your faithfulness to the skies.
Your righteousness is like the highest mountains,
your justice like the great deep.
You, LORD, preserve both people and animals.
How priceless is your unfailing love, O God!
People take refuge in the shadow of your wings.
They feast on the abundance of your house;
you give them drink from your river of delights.
For with you is the fountain of life;
in your light we see light.

PSALM 36:5–9 NIV

Jesus replied that people soon became thirsty again after drinking this water. "But the water I give them," he said, "becomes a perpetual spring within them, watering them forever with eternal life."

JOHN 4:13-14 TLB

A generous person will prosper;
whoever refreshes others will be refreshed.

PROVERBS 11: 25 NIV

"Let anyone who is thirsty come to me and drink. Whoever believes in me, as Scripture has said, rivers of living water will flow from within them."

JOHN 7:37-38 NIV

RELATIONSHIP

I am my beloved's, And his desire is toward me.

SONG OF SOLOMON 7:10 NKJV

We were also chosen to belong to him. God decided
to choose us long ago in keeping with his plan.
He works out everything to fit his plan and purpose.
We were the first to put our hope in Christ.
We were chosen to bring praise to his glory.

EPHESIANS 1:11–12 NIRV

My God is changeless in his love for me,
and he will come and help me.

PSALM 59:10 TLB

You make known to me the path of life;
you will fill me with joy in your presence,
with eternal pleasures at your right hand.

PSALM 16:11 NIV

"The LORD your God is living among you.
He is a mighty savior.
He will take delight in you with gladness.
With his love, he will calm all your fears.
He will rejoice over you with joyful songs."

ZEPHANIAH 3:17 NLT

My beloved speaks and says to me:
"Arise, my love, my beautiful one,
and come away,
for behold, the winter is past;
the rain is over and gone.
The flowers appear on the earth,
the time of singing has come."

SONG OF SOLOMON 2:10-12 ESV

RENEWAL

We shall not all sleep, but we shall all be changed.

1 CORINTHIANS 15:51 NKJV

The LORD is good to all,
and his mercy is over all that he has made.

PSALM 145:9 ESV

At one time you were dead in your sins.
Your desires controlled by sin were not circumcised.
But God gave you new life together with Christ.
He forgave us all our sins.

COLOSSIANS 2:13 NIRV

If anyone is in Christ, he is a new creation;
old things have passed away;
behold, all things have become new.

2 CORINTHIANS 5:17 NKJV

Praise the LORD!
Oh, give thanks to the LORD, for He is good!
For His mercy endures forever.

PSALM 106:1 NKJV

God was bringing the world back to himself
through Christ. He did not hold people's sins
against them. God has trusted us with the
message that people may be brought back to him.
So we are Christ's official messengers.
It is as if God were making his appeal through us.
Here is what Christ wants us to beg you to do.
Come back to God!

2 CORINTHIANS 5:19–20 NIRV

THIS IS THE WAY

When you turn to the right or when you turn to the left, your ears shall hear a word behind you, saying, "This is the way; walk in it."

ISAIAH 30:21 NRSV

We worry a lot about missing God's will. We are already convinced that his will is best for us—but what does that mean if we can't find what his will is?

As we think about life after high school or college, it's easy to stress about making the right choice. How can we be sure that what we are choosing is God's choice for our lives?

The beautiful part about being a child of God is that we are given the Holy Spirit who leads us into all truth. God promises that no matter what direction we need in life, we will hear his voice speaking to us and telling us where to go. We'll know in our spirits what he has in store for us.

Continue to practice hearing him through prayer and study of his Word. He'll lead you on the best path just like he said he would.

PRAYER:

God, I want to live your plan for my life because I know it's the best plan. Sometimes I worry that I'll miss out on what you want for me, but I know that you don't want to hide your will from me. I know that you are speaking to me. Help me to listen.

RESTORATION

Since we have been made right in God's sight by faith, we have peace with God because of what Jesus Christ our Lord has done for us. Because of our faith, Christ has brought us into this place of undeserved privilege where we now stand, and we confidently and joyfully look forward to sharing God's glory.

ROMANS 5:1–2 NLT

He has saved us and called us to a holy life—not because of anything we have done but because of his own purpose and grace.

2 TIMOTHY 1:9 NIV

"Let us praise the Lord, the God of Israel,
because he has come to help his people
and has given them freedom.
He has given us a powerful Savior."

LUKE 1:68-69 NCV

Dear brothers and sisters, we can boldly enter heaven's Most Holy Place because of the blood of Jesus. By his death, Jesus opened a new and life-giving way through the curtain into the Most Holy Place. And since we have a great High Priest who rules over God's house, let us go right into the presence of God with sincere hearts fully trusting him.

HEBREWS 10:19–22 NLT

REWARD

Without faith it is impossible to please God, because anyone who comes to him must believe that he exists and that he rewards those who earnestly seek him.

HEBREWS 11:6 NIV

Watch yourselves, so that you may not lose what we have worked for, but may win a full reward.

2 JOHN 1:8 ESV

Remember that the Lord will reward each one of us for the good we do.

EPHESIANS 6:8 NLT

"Look, I am coming soon! My reward is with me, and I will give to each person according to what they have done."

REVELATION 22:12 NIV

Do not lose the courage you had in the past, which has a great reward. You must hold on, so you can do what God wants and receive what he has promised.

HEBREWS 10:35-36 NCV

I have fought the good fight, I have finished the course, I have kept the faith; in the future there is laid up for me the crown of righteousness, which the Lord, the righteous Judge, will award to me on that day; and not only to me, but also to all who have loved His appearing.

2 TIMOTHY 4:7-8 NASB

ROYALTY

Because we are his children, God has sent the Spirit of his Son into our hearts, prompting us to call out, "Abba, Father." Now you are no longer a slave but God's own child. And since you are his child, God has made you his heir.

GALATIANS 4:6-7 NLT

As many as received Him, to them He gave the right to become children of God, even to those who believe in His name.

JOHN 1:12 NASB

"Love your enemies, do good to them, and lend to them without expecting to get anything back. Then your reward will be great, and you will be children of the Most High."

LUKE 6:35 NIV

See what great love the Father has lavished on us, that we should be called children of God! And that is what we are! The reason the world does not know us is that it did not know him. Dear friends, now we are children of God, and what we will be has not yet been made known. But we know that when Christ appears, we shall be like him, for we shall see him as he is.

1 JOHN 3:1-2 NIV

SAFER IN HIS HANDS

When I am afraid, I will put my trust in You.
In God, whose word I praise,
In God I have put my trust; I shall not be afraid.
What can mere man do to me?

PSALM 56:3-4 NASB

Trust isn't easy. Trust means letting go. It means giving up control. It means believing that someone else can handle something as well or better than we can.

Trust isn't usually our first reaction. Typically we want to hold on to the things that are valuable to us as tightly as we can—letting go of them is the last thing we want.

There is one person we can trust with everything we have: one person who can always handle it better than we can. God is trustworthy. He's never shown himself to be anything less. You can trust him with whatever situation comes your way. And you can trust him with your whole life.

When fear overtakes you and you want to take back control, remember that your life is far safer in God's hands than it would ever be in yours.

PRAYER:

Lord, I know that you are trustworthy. When it comes to actually placing my life in your hands, I get fearful. Give me peace and the knowledge that you are to be trusted completely. You've never let me down, and I know that you never will.

SATISFACTION

Because your love is better than life,
my lips will glorify you.
I will praise you as long as I live,
and in your name I will lift up my hands.
I will be fully satisfied as with the richest of foods;
with singing lips my mouth will praise you.

PSALM 63:3–5 NIV

God is able to provide you with every blessing in
abundance, so that by always having enough of
everything, you may share abundantly
in every good work.

2 CORINTHIANS 9:8 NRSV

The LORD is all I need. He takes care of me.
My share in life has been pleasant;
my part has been beautiful.

PSALM 16:5–6 NCV

The poor shall eat and be satisfied; all who see
the Lord shall find him and shall praise his name.
Their hearts shall rejoice with everlasting joy.

PSALM 22:26 TLB

"Give, and it will be given to you.
A good measure, pressed down, shaken together
and running over, will be poured into your lap.
For with the measure you use,
it will be measured to you."

LUKE 6:38 NIV

Whoever pursues righteousness and love
finds life, prosperity and honor.

PROVERBS 21:21 NIV

SECURITY

The everlasting God is your place of safety,
and his arms will hold you up forever.

DEUTERONOMY 33:27 NCV

Every good and perfect gift is from above, coming
down from the Father of the heavenly lights, who
does not change like shifting shadows.

JAMES 1:17 NIV

The grass withers,
And its flower falls away,
But the word of the LORD endures forever.

1 PETER 1:24–25 NKJV

In peace I will lie down and sleep,
for you alone, LORD,
make me dwell in safety.

PSALM 4:8 NIV

You are near, Lord,
and all your commands are true.
Long ago I learned from your statutes
that you established them to last forever.

PSALM 119:151–152 NIV

Our steps are made firm by the Lord,
when he delights in our way;
though we stumble, we shall not fall headlong,
for the Lord holds us by the hand.

PSALM 37:23–24 NRSV

STRENGTH

"My grace is sufficient for you, for My strength is made perfect in weakness." Therefore most gladly I will rather boast in my infirmities, that the power of Christ may rest upon me. For when I am weak, then I am strong.

2 CORINTHIANS 12:9 NKJV

In Your hand is power and might;
In Your hand it is to make great
And to give strength to all.

1 CHRONICLES 29:12 NKJV

Be strong in the Lord and in his mighty power.
Put on the full armor of God, so that you can
take your stand against the devil's schemes.

EPHESIANS 6:10–11 NIV

Have you never heard?
Have you never understood?
The LORD is the everlasting God,
the Creator of all the earth.
He never grows weak or weary.
No one can measure the depths of his understanding.
He gives power to the weak
and strength to the powerless.
Even youths will become weak and tired,
and young men will fall in exhaustion.
But those who trust in the LORD will find new strength.
They will soar high on wings like eagles.
They will run and not grow weary.
They will walk and not faint.

ISAIAH 40:28-31 NLT

SUPPORT

Whom have I in heaven but you?
And earth has nothing I desire besides you.
My flesh and my heart may fail,
but God is the strength of my heart
and my portion forever.

PSALM 73:25–26 NIV

The LORD is near to the brokenhearted
and saves the crushed in spirit.

PSALM 34:18 ESV

You, God, see the trouble of the afflicted;
you consider their grief and take it in hand.
The victims commit themselves to you;
you are the helper of the fatherless.

PSALM 10:14 NIV

Live as citizens of heaven, conducting yourselves in a manner worthy of the Good News about Christ... standing together with one spirit and one purpose, fighting together for the faith. Don't be intimidated in any way by your enemies. This will be a sign to them that you are going to be saved, even by God himself.

PHILIPPIANS 1:27–28 NLT

God will never forget the needy;
the hope of the afflicted will never perish.

PSALM 9:18 NIV

You are my hiding place;
You shall preserve me from trouble;
You shall surround me with songs of deliverance.

PSALM 32:7 NKJV

Be joyful in hope, patient in affliction, faithful in prayer.

ROMANS 12:12 NIV

Do you enjoy waiting? Most of us don't enjoy it, but what if we could? We spend much of our lives hoping, waiting, and praying for things that haven't yet happened. How great would it be if that time were joyful, filled with patience and faith?

This short verse in Romans is overflowing with encouragement for times of waiting. While you hope, be joyful. In other words, expect the thing you hope for. Anticipate it. If you're suffering, be patient. Relax, rest, and know your time of affliction will end. While you pray, be filled with faith. Believe in God's willingness to grant your heart's desires, and continue to bring them before him.

Try it, and see if your perspective on waiting changes.

PRAYER:

Lord, waiting is so hard! Whether I'm in a hurry or afraid what I wait for may not happen, I find myself anxious and impatient. Thank you for this verse and its reminder to slow down and anticipate the time you'll fulfill my longing and answer my prayers. Fill me with faith as I wait and hope.

TRUSTWORTHINESS

Listen, for I will speak of excellent things,
And from the opening of my lips
will come right things;
For my mouth will speak truth.

PROVERBS 8:6–7 NKJV

A gossip goes around telling secrets, but those who
are trustworthy can keep a confidence.

PROVERBS 11:13 NLT

You must remain faithful to the things you have
been taught. You know they are true, for you know
you can trust those who taught you. You have been
taught the holy Scriptures from childhood, and they
have given you the wisdom to receive the salvation
that comes by trusting in Christ Jesus.

2 TIMOTHY 3:14–15 NLT

The Lord detests lying lips,
but he delights in people who are trustworthy.

PROVERBS 12:22 NIV

Show yourself in all respects to be a model of good works, and in your teaching show integrity, dignity, and sound speech that cannot be condemned, so that an opponent may be put to shame, having nothing evil to say about us.

TITUS 2:7-8 ESV

"One who is faithful in a very little
is also faithful in much."

LUKE 16:10 ESV

TRUTH

Truthful words stand the test of time,
but lies are soon exposed.

PROVERBS 12:19 NLT

"When he, the Spirit of truth, comes,
he will guide you into all the truth."

JOHN 16:13 NIV

"Everyone who does evil hates the light, and will not
come into the light for fear that their deeds will be
exposed. But whoever lives by the truth comes into
the light, so that it may be seen plainly that what
they have done has been done in the sight of God."

JOHN 3:20–21 NIV

You desire truth in the innermost being, And in the
hidden part You will make me know wisdom.

PSALM 51:6 NASB

The very essence of your words is truth;
all your just regulations will stand forever.

PSALM 119:160 NLT

His merciful kindness is great toward us,
And the truth of the LORD endures forever.
Praise the LORD!

PSALM 117:2 NKJV

Send out your light and your truth;
let them lead me;
let them bring me to your holy hill
and to your dwelling.

PSALM 43:3 NRSV

UNDERSTANDING

You know what I long for, Lord;
you hear my every sigh.

PSALM 38:9 NLT

"My sheep hear my voice, and I know them, and
they follow me. I give them eternal life, and they
will never perish, and no one will snatch them out
of my hand."

JOHN 10:27-28 ESV

God is not unjust; he will not overlook your work
and the love that you showed for his sake in
serving the saints, as you still do.

HEBREWS 6:10 NRSV

Great is our Lord and mighty in power;
his understanding has no limit.

PSALM 147:5 NIV

For we do not have a high priest who is unable to empathize with our weaknesses, but we have one who has been tempted in every way, just as we are—yet he did not sin.

HEBREWS 4:15 NIV

"As the heavens are higher than the earth,
So are My ways higher than your ways
And My thoughts higher than your thoughts."

ISAIAH 55:9 NASB

Blessed is the one who finds wisdom,
and the one who gets understanding.

PROVERBS 3:13 ESV

Our purpose is to please God, not people.
He alone examines the motives of our hearts.

1 THESSALONIANS 2:4 NLT

I remind you to fan into flame the gift of God for God gave us a spirit not of fear but of power and love and self-control.

2 TIMOTHY 1:6-7 ESV

Any new situation can be daunting. A new city. A new job. A new group of friends. A new adventure. A new opportunity. Any of these could cause our knees to buckle and our hearts to race.

Sometimes we need boldness for the concrete and tangible fears we face: an angry family member, a disgruntled friend, a dropped responsibility. Maybe we need boldness to defend the weak and rise up for the forgotten. Sometimes we simply need boldness to do what we know is right.

Many times, we want to cower and hide, but hiding doesn't make fears disappear. Instead, they are allowed to fester and grow. Before we know it, fear is taking control of our lives. You may wish that you were braver. You *can* be. God has equipped you with everything you need to conquer any situation. He has given you the weapons to fight with—chin up and shoulders squared.

You never have to go into any situation afraid. You can have full assurance that God will give you the boldness you need in the exact moment you need it.

PRAYER:

God, you made me a warrior. Warriors don't run from scary situations; they march forward and battle on. Show me just how brave I can be when I depend on you.

VICTORY

Thanks be to God! He gives us the victory through our Lord Jesus Christ.

1 CORINTHIANS 15:57 NIV

Can anything ever separate us from Christ's love? Does it mean he no longer loves us if we have trouble or calamity, or are persecuted, or hungry, or destitute, or in danger, or threatened with death? No, despite all these things, overwhelming victory is ours through Christ, who loved us.

ROMANS 8:35, 37 NLT

Thanks be to God, who always leads us in triumph in Christ, and manifests through us the sweet aroma of the knowledge of Him in every place.

2 CORINTHIANS 2:14 NASB

In fact, this is love for God: to keep his commands. And his commands are not burdensome, for everyone born of God overcomes the world. This is the victory that has overcome the world, even our faith. Who is it that overcomes the world? Only the one who believes that Jesus is the Son of God.

1 JOHN 5:3-5 NIV

Commit your actions to the LORD,
and your plans will succeed.

PROVERBS 16:3 NLT

Victory comes from you, O LORD.
May you bless your people.

PSALM 3:8 NLT

WHOLENESS

The LORD rewarded me for doing right;
he restored me because of my innocence.
For I have kept the ways of the Lord;
I have not turned from my God to follow evil.
I have followed all his regulations;
I have never abandoned his decrees.
I am blameless before God;
I have kept myself from sin.
The LORD rewarded me for doing right.
He has seen my innocence.

PSALM 18:20-24 NLT

He will take our weak mortal bodies and change
them into glorious bodies like his own, using the
same power with which he will bring everything
under his control.

PHILIPPIANS 3:21 NLT

All praise to God, the Father of our Lord Jesus Christ. It is by his great mercy that we have been born again, because God raised Jesus Christ from the dead. Now we live with great expectation, and we have a priceless inheritance—an inheritance that is kept in heaven for you, pure and undefiled, beyond the reach of change and decay. And through your faith, God is protecting you by his power until you receive this salvation, which is ready to be revealed on the last day for all to see.

1 PETER 1:3-5 NLT

"For you who fear my name, the sun of righteousness shall rise with healing in its wings."

MALACHI 4:2 ESV

WISDOM

The unfolding of your words gives light;
it gives understanding to the simple.

PSALM 119:130 NIV

What we have received is not the spirit of the
world, but the Spirit who is from God, so that we
may understand what God has freely given us.

1 CORINTHIANS 2:12 NIV

Be filled with the knowledge of His will in all
spiritual wisdom and understanding, so that you
will walk in a manner worthy of the Lord... and
increasing in the knowledge of God.

COLOSSIANS 1:9-10 NASB

Do not be unwise,
but understand what the will of the Lord is.

EPHESIANS 5:17 NKJV

The wisdom from above is first of all pure. It is also peace loving, gentle at all times, and willing to yield to others. It is full of mercy and good deeds. It shows no favoritism and is always sincere.

JAMES 3:17 NLT

Listen carefully to wisdom;
set your mind on understanding.
Cry out for wisdom,
and beg for understanding.
Search for it like silver,
and hunt for it like hidden treasure.
Then you will understand respect for the LORD,
and you will find that you know God.

PROVERBS 2:2–5 NCV

A GOOD LEADER

"I am the good shepherd. The good shepherd
lays down his life for the sheep."

JOHN 10:11 NIV

What do you look for in a leader? To bring others
into a relationship with Christ, we have to become
leaders ourselves. One of the best examples we
could ever ask for in leadership was Jesus himself—
and he called himself a good shepherd. There was
good reason for this.

Though a shepherd was not a job that many aspired
to, it called for special skills. A shepherd had to
guide his flock of sheep without scaring them into
submission. Sheep are known to make poor choices
when operating under fear. Shepherds needed to
nourish, comfort, lead, correct, and protect their

sheep. And most importantly, a good shepherd would encourage those in his care to follow his example and stay with him.

Are you a leader for Christ's kingdom? As you enter a new chapter in your life, are you encouraging others to follow your example, comforting them in times of need and correcting them gently when the situation calls for it?

PRAYER:

Lord, please help me to display good leadership in my life. I want to model myself after you, the good shepherd, and care for others by leading them to you.

WORRY

"Which of you by worrying can add a single hour to his life's span?"

LUKE 12:25 NASB

Don't worry about anything; instead, pray about everything. Tell God what you need, and thank him for all he has done. Then you will experience God's peace, which exceeds anything we can understand. His peace will guard your hearts and minds as you live in Christ Jesus.

PHILIPPIANS 4:6–7 NLT

If people's thinking is controlled by the sinful self, there is death. But if their thinking is controlled by the Spirit, there is life and peace.

ROMANS 8:6 NCV

Worry weighs a person down;
an encouraging word cheers a person up.

PROVERBS 12:25 NLT

"Do not worry about your life, what you will eat
or drink; or about your body, what you will wear.
Is not life more than food, and the body more
than clothes? Look at the birds of the air; they
do not sow or reap or store away in barns, and
yet your heavenly Father feeds them. Are you not
much more valuable than they?"

MATTHEW 6:25–26 NIV

May the Lord of peace himself give you peace at
all times in every way.

2 THESSALONIANS 3:16 ESV

BroadStreet Publishing Group LLC
Racine, Wisconsin, USA
Broadstreetpublishing.com

Bible Promises for Graduates
© 2017 by BroadStreet Publishing

ISBN 978-1-4245-5459-1 (navy faux)
ISBN 978-1-4245-5460-7 (pink faux)
ISBN 978-1-4245-5461-4 (gray faux)
ISBN 978-1-4245-5462-1 (purple faux)

Design by Chris Garborg | www.garborgdesign.com
Compiled by Michelle Winger | www.literallyprecise.com

Printed in China

17   18   19   20   21   22   23   7   6   5   4   3   2   1